The Book
of the
Lord's Wisdom

The Grace Addition

GREATNESS QUIROZ

ISBN 979-8-89112-090-7 (Paperback)
ISBN 979-8-89112-091-4 (Digital)

Covenant Books
11661 Hwy 707
Murrells Inlet, SC 29576
www.covenantbooks.com

You know, at the beginning of writing this book, the Lord told us that we would write this book and that it would be deliverance for all those who sought it. He told me that we would write a book of wisdom and great knowledge. I then questioned it in excitement and asked Him if it would be just like Solomon's book of wisdom, and then He said, "No! It's nothing like Solomon's," but in a sterner voice. LOL. This was His comment to me. Solomon is not the wisest person who ever lived; Jesus is, and now He is one with us. Amen.

He said that Solomon was the wisest man of his time. He could teach the world how to be successful in all things with God. He could not teach with the wisdom we carry because Christ had not gone to the cross yet. Solomon taught others how to be successful, and we now have the wisdom within us to teach others how to already be successful, be like God, and rule everything as lords. Solomon did not have the wisdom and knowledge of anything that has to do with Jesus and Jesus reigning in us; it was not available then, so it was never given to him to teach like we can. Solomon was still under *dos* and *don'ts* so that's what his wisdom consisted of: <u>teaching</u> everyone what not to do and what to do to have a successful life following the Lord.

Grace is higher than the law, so the wisdom that comes with grace is higher than the wisdom that came with the law. So when we are in complete oneness with the Lord Jesus, we are then wiser than anyone before Jesus. We are the new and better creations that didn't even exist in Solomon's time. Amen.

Because it is the Lord speaking, if you are of the same spirit, the Lord will affirm it with you even if you didn't know before. It's kind of like a light bulb turning on above your head. Remember that Jesus is always with you once you are born again into this new creation. He is one with you. Many would even agree that He is the best part of you. LOL. So no matter where you are, talk to Him. You don't have to get into some super spiritual mood just for Him to answer. That is the Old Testament's way. We are now under grace.

At first, it may be weird because it is new to you, but after a while, He will be more real to you than your own spouse. He will even be that best friend to you who has no flaws. He will make you laugh when you're feeling down, and He's always there to put a smile on your face when you feel like nothing or no one can. He loves you more than you know. Amen.

Wisdom is for everyone in general.

Knowledge is mainly according to the call that He has given you and the things that you will need on the way there and forward.

He is always there to give you both. Seek Him.

Keynote: When you begin to see more favor in your life, which you will because of My presence with you, don't think you are better than others and forget that it is only because you are at a higher level of grace (my undeserved favor in your life).

Then pride will sneak in.

The Holy Spirit is the bridge from you to Jesus. He is the one Who brings it forth and teaches you. He is one with the Lord also, therefore being one with you too. "I teach you what the Lord wants to teach you," says the Holy Spirit.

Will deliver. Amen.

Picture this: He is the one Who lowers the pail into the well to bring up to you the living water, which is Jesus. Now you can receive what He (Jesus) has for you. That's why it's important to keep your well clean. Pray in the spirit, amen.

I will make you great in the sight of men.

What He meant here is that He won't just make you great. He is saying that once you become one with Him, His greatness will show in you because He is the one Who is great in the sight of men. Amen.

A prophet is one with the Lord, and many of my people are one with the Lord. This is the prophet's job: to lead people to be one with the Lord in a more intimate way, with more power and more affirmation. That's why when a prophet speaks something into the earth, it happens because it is the Lord speaking it into the earth (not the same as prophecy). I am here to get people from where they are to where they need to be. Amen.

We are a new creation that has never existed. Back then, they were one with God. Now as a new creation, we are one with God. When you are actually one with the Lord, greatness takes place.

The Holy Spirit in the old times could only come down for a moment and then leave just like the angels. "I was forbidden to stay here," says the Lord. God cannot coexist with men. We are nasty and full of sin. God cannot live with sin, and the Holy Spirit and the angels had to be sent.

Jesus jumped without being sent. That was forbidden and the end of the law. Now He can live down here because He cleansed it with His blood and brought us back to the Father. That's why we pray, "Your Kingdom come, Your will be done on earth as it is in heaven. Amen." It starts in heaven and then happens here.

In heaven, He overcame the law with love, and that's why the law down here was also completed with love. "This is my Son whom I am well pleased *in*." He used love to conquer all and bring us back to our Father. Not then, but now we can cry out, "Abba, Father!"

Love is the greatest force in nature. It conquers all. Amen.

Exodus 2:23–24 confirms that the Lord can hear our cries in heaven. It reads, "The children of Israel groaned because of the bondage, and they cried out, their cry came up to God because of the bondage, so God heard their groaning, and God remembered his covenant with Abraham, Isaac, and Jacob." This confirms Jesus hearing the cries of the people from heaven. Which heaven, you may ask? That is entirely up to you *in* the Lord.

Jesus is God and man; this is why He can be in oneness with us.

As I was writing this, I saw my journal light up, so I looked up, and the Lord was in front of me with a group of about fifteen to twenty angels. Their combined light was so bright that I had to squint just to look in that direction. I asked to confirm what I am seeing. "Lord, are those angels?"

He said, "Yes, Oscar. I wanted you to see them to know that you have a full army watching over and assisting you on our journey." Then they assured me that they were with me and that we would go forward together. The Lord said that they will always be with us now. "They are always with you, Oscar. I just had their presence manifested so that you can see."

"So even if I can't see them, they are always there?"

"Of course," says the Lord. "They hear Me speak when you speak. They will anticipate My will. They make sure that My will is getting through [being done] and that nothing is in the way. Amen. They go before you, Oscar, and make sure your way is clear. They are your shield. You know, I've always been here for you, Oscar. All things are going to change for you. Today is a good day that I have made. Forward from here, you will see my awesomeness in and around your life. I will always be here with you, and you will always be blessed. Amen. That's just one perk that comes with the job."

All good comes to those who have trusted God.

"I am always at your side. Do My will, and everything else will just fall into your lap. Be of good cheer. I am and always will be in you. Amen. We are one, and we will always be one. My love for you is great. Never forget that, Oscar. I'm never leaving your side, nor am I leaving those who come to Me from here forward. Amen. This is the best day I've had with you. I enjoyed this. I enjoyed being with you. Thank you, Oscar, I love you."

I am blessed because the Lord is with me. It comes with the territory. There's no way around it because it is Who He is. These have been the best <u>day</u> of my whole life, and it's only going to get greater. I *now* know what it is like to be ridiculously happy!

This probably was the most emotional day out of all of them. Just knowing that the trip had come to an end was tough, I felt as if I had been in heaven these days and *know* it was time for me to go back to the world.

During <u>these</u> times, the Lord keeps encouraging me and letting me know that this is not over and that He will always be like this with me from now on. Thank you is all I keep saying over and over.

Information of All

In Luke 9:1–6, Jesus sends out the disciples to do His will, and He tells them not to take any of their food or money and basically to stay at others' homes and allow them to feed them and make sure their needs are provided. He also says here to shake off the very dust from their feet if they do not receive them as a testimony against them. God is always giving His children an opportunity to be blessed because He wants that for us all. The disciples did not need any of that. They already had the money for an inn. They had food. All their needs were met, but the Lord wanted to bless the people there in more ways than just getting the word. So He knew that whatever they gave to the disciples, they were giving it to Him, therefore allowing them to plant great seed into good ground (Jesus). That way, they could prosper in more ways than one.

So when He instructs a ministry to ask for donations, I guarantee you that it's not because they need it; it's because you do.

He wants to see your heart and bring great reward into your lives by giving to Him. Amen.

"Always know that wherever you go, all of heaven is with you." Amen.

We are one and they follow in Me. Never be troubled by this truth, you are safe and protected. Amen. In this truth, no weapon ever formed against you will <u>ever</u> prosper. AMEN. *Know this!*

A little after we left *the house*, I began to notice that I was beginning to function and do things as I was doing beforehand. It troubled me because I felt as if I was alone. So in my troubled thoughts, I journaled like before and asked the Lord, "Lord Jesus, can you please tell me what's happening to me?"

"I'm with you, Oscar. We are one. Don't be troubled. I need you to know that I am God. You can't make choices alone, Oscar. We are one. There is no *I* in a team. I am with you. We will do good, but we have to do it together."

"*Yes!*" I say, "*I don't want You to be that small voice coming from within! I want us to speak together, walk, and see, and everything in between. I never want You, Jesus, to be one within me speaking. I want us to be ONE in all things together. We are one soul and one body. Amen!*"

This is what we wanted and became. Amen.

The Lord's Wisdom

The beginning

When you and the Lord are <u>one</u>, you can't mess up because He is in charge. Amen. When you are <u>with</u> the Lord, and He speaks to you from within or even on the outside, you have a choice. Do I listen and follow, or don't I?

Don't make schedules. They put condemnation on those who can't keep them, and they take the focus off of the Lord.

Samuel knew this. He didn't keep schedules. Saul panicked because, to him, Samuel was late. So he did things himself and told Samuel that he thought that he would not show up because he was late. Samuel was not late; he was where the Lord wanted him to be, <u>not on schedule.</u> This also tested Saul's heart on his faith, obedience, and patience—all characteristics of the Lord's heart.

If you are truly free and are not bound by schedules, it is another form of the law. Be here or do that is what the schedules say. In other words, do this or be here, or else, there will be consequences. Is that not the law in another tense to keep people from being free? Now that schedule has you in bondage, and if you slip, condemnation hits, or even worse, punishment in some form.

If you are one with the perfect one, how can you mess up? As one, you are perfect in Christ. Amen.

If you have to maintain, you never *knew* what you had to begin with. Amen.

For the Lord will give you all the desires of your heart. once you are one with Him, and they fall in line with His will. Amen.

You are one <u>now</u> one soul and one body. Amen.

More truth is being revealed to *us* because of the veil thinning out, because of His greatness (presence). The enemy is panicking because it is harder to keep this truth from getting to us. *We are conquerors. Amen.*

When you are one with the Lord, He still wants us to enjoy all things just as it is written, but He says that there is a right way to do it. He won't let you get hooked or get to a place where you are putting too much focus toward something other than Him. Therefore, you cannot mess up. Amen.

When you are one with Jesus, you don't have to pray for things like having more confidence or courage. "When they are One with Me, they are already confident and courageous." Amen. You don't need confidence; you need Jesus.

He is the whole package. Declaring that you are one with Jesus means you are everything He is. Amen. Why ask for the apple when you can receive an apple tree?

Too many people waste too much time declaring by faith one weakness at a time. <u>When they could just declare oneness with Jesus,</u> everything else already comes with Him.

The more Jesus is added to anything, the more beautiful it becomes. Amen.

When you are one with the Lord, He will use you to create something beautiful wherever you are at. Amen.

Great things come to those who trust in the Lord. Amen.

No matter what you see in front of you or around you, the Lord will use it for His good pleasure. Amen.

When you are one with the Lord, He will just start creating wherever you are. Amen.

Whatever you touch will prosper. Amen.

"Because I Am one with you," says the Lord. Amen.

The Lord will use anything around you and make it beautiful.

THAT'S JUST WHO HE IS. AMEN.

Whenever the Lord is speaking through you or writing, do not try to go back and replace words that He spoke so that it would make more sense. He spoke it that way for a reason. Amen.

When you are one with the Lord, you do not need to try and get in His presence; you are already there. *Just be* you. You are one with Him. Amen.

Everything has a perfect spot, even if at first it seems corrupted and useless. You will soon see <u>*there*</u> was a spot for it the whole time.

Just be <u>patient,</u> and you will see. Amen.

Be like a child and always find something to play with and enjoy. A child is always excited and finding new things to do. They are always joyful. *Be the same.* Amen. That is the joy of the Lord. Amen.

To a child, everything they do is beautiful no matter what. JUST BE YOU. Amen.

Some things that are so simple in life, you will find that they have the most beauty. They are glorious. Amen.

It is beautiful because you created it with the Lord.

Be in oneness with Him, and you shall see.

The Lord loves everything and anything He creates, even if you see it as different and does not fit in or is right. He still takes great joy in seeing His work of art. Amen.

If only you could see how excited He gets just to put two Legos together. It is something of pure beauty to Him because it was something He made.

The Joy of the Lord Is My Strength

I sat here laughing as the Lord and I *were* building so many masterpieces together with the Legos.

It was the most fun I've ever had with the Lord. I loved it. Such a perfect day.

You just can't compare this joy and love. He is great. Amen! Thank You, Lord, is what I speak.

I look at some of these pieces and think to myself, *Some of these pieces don't even look like they have purpose. they're just there.* But the Lord sees them as something beautiful, and you <u>stare</u> at them in awe and love because He made them.

I love that He allowed me to see as He sees. Thank You, Lord.

We operate, we move, and we function in His love.

When you see someone who may appear slow to you, they are actually an example of how you can still be in a mature body and still enjoy life as a child. The Lord has set them all around us so that everyone can see what it's like. Watch them closely. They have no cares, and they love everything. "I love them so much," says my Lord Jesus. Amen.

"People give Satan way too much credit," says the Lord. "I made them that way so that they could be your example. Love them as I DO, amen."

Don't you notice that the people who normally take care of these people are some of the most loving and caring people? They have a childlike joy in them because of always being around them. Do you not see what an example they are for your life? Others say they are slow, but I say they are actually one step closer. "Follow their example."

They bring so much joy to everyone around them, and naturally, you tend to imitate them. Isn't that a reward in itself?

All good things come to those who trust in the Lord. Nowhere here does it say for us to go to these good things. When you are one with the Lord, good things come to you. It's almost as if they just fall into your laps wherever you are at. *Be one with the Lord. Amen.*

Seek first His righteousness and His kingdom, and everything else will just be added to you.

It will come to you because that's Who He is.

Amen.

When you are one with the Lord, you will see that you just happen to know things all the time, without even thinking about it because He knows all things. Amen.

When you get to a place of being one with the Lord, you will notice that you don't have to go to a *quiet* place anymore to hear Him. You are one, remember.

When you are one with the Lord, no mysteries will be withheld from you. How can Jesus keep something from you if you are one with Him. His secrets are your secrets, amen?

This is why Scripture says that not even Jesus knows the hour that the Lord will come. If He did, we would know because you are one with Him. Amen.

When the Father says something to Jesus, He is also saying it to us. Amen. <u>Understand this</u>.

Two people who are not in unity are unequally yoked. If one is one with the Lord and another is not, this won't work because both of them are of a different spirit. If they are both one, everything will be in perfect harmony because of having Jesus leading them both. Amen.

No matter how you look or how you dress, you will always be blessed when you are in line with the Lord. Amen.

The Lord will give you the desires of your heart because you are blessed. Not by anything else.

And you are blessed when *you* are one with Him. Amen.

Everything good comes all the time when you are one with the Lord. Amen. Sometimes the Lord will withhold things from you that He has stored *up* for you.

He waits till you are one with Him to give it to you.

When you are one with the Lord, you will just begin to speak in your spiritual language as you go.

"It will just come out as you go."

When you are one with the Lord, everything you ever need to know is already in you. You just need to remember.

The Holy Spirit will bring it to remembrance when it is needed. Amen? You and the Lord share one mind and one body. Amen. Everything you will ever need to know is now there. He is all-knowing. Amen.

Being one with the Lord is complete freedom.

We are everything He is. Isn't that exciting!

Amen.

When you are one with the Lord, you will always be able to discern what is of the same Spirit and what is not. Amen.

When you are one with the Lord, you won't have to seek after having more of Christ in you anymore. You will have the fullness of the Lord <u>now</u> dwelling in you. Amen? Complete oneness! Amen.

In this truth, you will know that you are one with the Lord. Yes and amen.

Wherever your foot treads, it is now holy ground. This means that the Lord has now treaded there. Amen.

Whatever you touch, the Lord has touched.

Amen? Blessed it is to be touched by the Lord. Amen.

Greatness is love, amen? You can't have one without the other. "We are one." amen.

Time itself *does not exist* to the Lord. Time does not exist to greatness. We are everywhere and everyone at the same time. We are one. "Wherever you look, you see Me," says the Lord. "I am at all places at once." Do you not see that we are one and the same?

We are the same. We are one. Amen.

Even if things don't make sense, it does not mean that nothing is happening. I am always there. Amen.

I am one with you. You, too, are always there.

This is why God said, "We are of one body. Amen. I am you, and you are Me. Amen? Do you not see that? I am the greatest part of you all. We are all in unity, one. Amen."

The Holy Spirit will always be <u>here</u>. Being one with the Lord Jesus requires that we die to ourselves. Amen.

To be one with the Lord will come with all His attributes. Amen.

Becoming one with the Lord takes great sacrifice, but the reward at the end will be greater. Amen. *Everlasting joy.* Amen!

To be one with the Lord is to be absent from all the garbage that keeps you from Him. Amen.

The Holy Spirit cleans out that garbage when we speak in tongues. When you're one with the Lord, the garbage stays out because Jesus is one with you. Amen.

Jesus will not live in the garbage. He is pure. Amen.

It is very important to know this truth.

This is the foundation of oneness with the Lord Jesus. Amen.

Patience is a strong key to this all as well.

Good comes to those who diligently wait upon the Lord. Patience. Amen.

Even through our transformation, we *must* continue to trust the Lord at all times.

Amen.

Greatness will come *upon* those who trust the Lord and those who diligently seek after Him. Amen.

"You must desire to be in oneness with the Lord Jesus." Amen. *Am in.*

"With this truth, greatness will just fall into your lap. Amen."

"It will become you." Amen.

When you are one with the Lord, just be you, and everything you do with the Lord will just fall in place—all in perfect order, all in perfect time.

Amen.

The joy of the Lord is my strength. Nowhere here does it say that your joy is your strength. "Your joy is limited." Amen?

The joy of the Lord is everlasting, eternal.

Amen.

When you are one with the Lord, you will begin to witness all His beauty in all His creation. Amen. *He is beauty.* Amen.

The Lord takes great joy in watching us explore. He wants us to see His beauty in all things. Amen.

It is, even more, greater to explore in oneness with the Lord and see everything for how He *sees* it. Amen. "*Beautiful.*" Amen.

All that Jesus is, we are. Amen. Get this truth, and you will be set free. Amen.

When you are one with the Lord, you will see that everything is always in motion. Everything is always moving. Amen.

When you are one, all good things come to those who trust in the Lord. Amen.

Complete unity is a sign of oneness. Amen.

When you are in oneness, no weapon formed against you will ever prosper. Amen.

The Lord is perfect in all things. Amen.

When you understand this truth, everything else just falls into place. Amen.

"'If you are one with Me,' says the Lord, 'All things will always go according to plan. My Greatness will show in and around your life.'" Amen.

"I am your strength, I am you." Amen. "We are one," says the Lord. Amen.

The Lord Jesus is the greatest of all gifts. Seek Him, and everything else will be added to you because He is everything. Amen.

If you can believe this truth, all things will be added to you. You will be all that He is and more! Amen.

When we are all in unity, great things tend to take place. Unity is powerful. It is a greater oneness. Amen. Understand this truth. Amen.

When you are in unity, <u>anything</u> else that is not of the Lord will just fall away from you and your life.

"If you are one with Me, you will know everything *about Me* and My <u>nature</u>." Amen. Confession is powerful. This is why we say amen. (So be it.)

This is the greatness of the Lord. Amen. And His ministry. We are one.

Confirmation verses

In 1 Corinthians 13:10,

> But when that which is Perfect has come, then that which is in part will be done away. Jesus is the perfect Here, God is love. Amen.

In 1 Corinthians 13:2,

> And though I have the gift of prophecy, and understand all Mysteries and all knowledge, and though I have all Faith so that I could remove mountains, but have not love, I am nothing.

Paul knew about being in oneness with the Lord because the Lord is perfect in all things, and He is all knowing. Now Paul was too perfect and all knowing because of his being in oneness with the Lord. Perfect love casts out all fear. Amen.

Only Jesus is perfect love, and that perfect love only can be acquired by becoming one with the Perfect One. Amen.

When you are one, you are always in each other's presence. Amen.

"How can you be one with another and say you are not in their presence? That does not make any sense."

When you are one with the Lord, you don't even have to try anything. Just be you. Amen.

Everything has no choice but to come to us. Amen.

As one, we are everything and everywhere. Amen. Enjoy this greatness. Amen.

When you are one, you will know when your time here is finished.

The Church's Parables

In John 10:34, "Jesus answered them; 'Is it not written in <u>Your</u> Law,' I said, 'You are gods'?" (referring to Psalm 82).

Many times, the Lord will give you an opportunity to do something the right way to not harm yourself. Amen.

On your journey, you will notice that you will give according to where and how the Lord wants to give. Amen.

The Lord is a giver. Amen.

Great things come to those who trust in the Lord. Amen.

When you are one with the Lord, you will know Him at His highest peak; therefore, you, too, will begin to know you. Amen.

You have no reason to ever worry or stress about anything in life. Amen. The Lord is always with you.

Any type of fear will drive away the Lord and His love.

I am love. I am life. I am the truth. Amen.

This is the truth. Amen.

You will always be one with the Lord because you are already one with the Lord. Amen.

All good things come to those who trust the Lord. Amen. Jesus is the greatest of all things that will come to those who all trust in the Lord. Amen.

We as one are the living water. Amen. We give to others so that they will never thirst again. Amen. We are that solution. Amen.

To be absent from the body is to be present with the Lord. Amen.

In this truth, you will still experience two deaths just like before. Now, you will first die to your body to be present with the Lord in oneness here on earth.

Then following the second death, you will be absent from your physical body to be permanently present with the Lord our God. Amen.

Just as we imitate our Father, our God, all creation also imitates us. To them, we are their God and Father. Amen.

All great things have no choice but to rise. Amen. We are those great things. Amen.

We are greatness. Amen.

As we conquer in life, we rise. Amen.

"Can you not see that we are already conquerors? Amen.

Don't tap into something that you already are. Amen.

I am the anointing. Amen.

When you are one with the Lord, you will love everyone and everything with one heart—His heart. Amen. The greatest kind of love.

When the Lord loves, He either loves something with a greater kind of love than we can imagine or He won't love at all. He does not love something more or less than others. He only knows <u>one</u> kind of love—the greatest kind. Amen.

Good things come to those who He loves. Amen.

Do you know that He loves you?

You can't trust someone who you don't know loves you. So therefore with no trust comes little to no faith.

Do you not see this? Amen.

Love is powerful. The more of His love you can understand, the more of His love you can send out. Amen.

There are three levels of spirituality after you are born again. There is the milk stage, followed by the meat stage of maturity, and then followed by the buffet stage, which is *complete* maturity. "<u>Oneness is perfection in the Lord.</u>" Amen.

Even under grace, the tithe is of great value. Its sole purpose is to break the bondage that it has over you. You can't be a lover of money and of God. To be one with the Lord, the Lord will require that you die to your trust in money and live all for Him. Amen.

The tithe will do that for you. It has its purpose, and it is a good one necessary for you. Amen.

Those who greet at the front line of the church and who are called to greet must be strong in love and heart. Amen.

They are the front-line soldiers who must have love to combat all those who are entering from the outside forces. Amen.

They are the ones who experience all of the hell that comes in from the outside. It is their love that will break the bondages of others. That same love is also their shield that will fend off all the darkness from attaching itself to them. This is why they must be strong in love.

They are the ones who get to strike first way before these hurt and destroyed people even get to praise and worship, and then the prayers come and then the word that completes the blow. Amen.

Greeters, be strong and conquer with the greatest kind of love—"My love," says the Lord. Amen.

When you are one with the Lord, He will become your life source. Everything else will just fall away and only be used for enjoyment. Amen.

Whatever the Lord instructs you to do will be according to the faith you have in Him and yourself. Amen.

When you are alone, you will discover mysteries about *yourself* and *your* life that you did not know before. Amen.

Solitude without distractions is of great necessity in OUR lives. Amen. Discover Jesus here. Aмen.

Correction is a beautiful gift. Welcome it.

It does not matter who gets intimate with the Lord and gets to speak. The message afterward will be the same. We are one. Amen.

In these times that we are in, Satan will use the truth to fight you off because of more truth coming in. He will use it to his advantage and come as an angel of light, deceiving those into thinking they can do all things without the Son of God. It will be the truth, but it's a false truth that will name you Antichrist.

The verse, "Many hands make light work," is good for not only your prosperity but also theirs. Amen.

When you help someone out, you are also helping yourself out, even if you can't see it at the moment. Amen.

A servant's heart brings great joy to both sides. Amen. It is well rewarded. Amen.

Greatness is one of these rewards. Amen.

"We are greatness." Amen.

Grace is the most powerful substance on earth. *No* <u>matter</u> what you do or say, the Lord's grace will still be upon you. Amen.

Grace is beautiful. Amen.

In all things, stay focused on the Lord Jesus. He is one with our Father and the Holy Spirit. Therefore, by staying focused on Him, you now, in return, are one with the Father, Son, and the Holy Spirit. Amen.

The best commandment yet. All good things come to those who have become one with the Lord God. Amen.

When you become one with the Lord, you will always conquer all things, even if you're not aware of it being done. Amen.

We are conquerors. That's just who we are. Amen.

The act of warfare is simply putting something greater than what was already there. Amen.

The verse, "Thy kingdom come, on Earth as it is in heaven," will be a reality once you are in complete oneness with the Lord. Amen. All the ways of heaven will now be a way of life for you. Amen.

If you discover that you are not yet in oneness, it suggests that there is more that you would need to depart from. Amen.

When you become one with the Lord, you will begin to know Him by His character and not so much by His Word.

To know the Lord and His character is to know yourselves. Amen.

Do not depend on others as a source; depend on the Lord, and He will be your only source through others. Amen.

Don't let yourself get dependent on the vessel and forget where everything is really coming from. Amen.

Beware of the enemy that destroys the revelation that you receive by putting a screen in front of you. Too much screen time will bring confusion and instability to you and your emotions. Amen.

Being in complete oneness is now being perfected. Amen.

From here, you can now reign as kings and queens. Amen.

You do not have to wait till you go to heaven to reign. This is a lie to contain you from the enemy.

Now when you are one in perfection, you can now bring heaven onto you. Amen.

To grow, it does not matter how much water is given to you but how much of it is consumed. Amen.

WE must not try and get all the word and teaching to ourselves if we are not in a position to <u>inhale</u> it. Amen.

Be wise. The enemy will always try to sell you something that you already have. Amen. Remember this.

Just <u>being</u> is the greatest way of bringing in all that you have been believing in prayer. Amen. Just be you. Amen.

When you tell someone to be healed, their body has to listen to you because you are the controller of the universe. Amen.

Picture this. You have many little soldiers or little nanites inside of your bloodstream, awaiting your order as you command them to.

They are powerful and stronger than you have ever known them to be. Amen.

When you are one with the Lord, you will see life through a whole different lens. Amen.

You will see life for its beauty with love, joy, and great compassion. Amen.

"The world is beautiful, and many do not see that I am within it all." Amen.

ENJOY LIFE, and ENJOY IT TO THE FULLEST.

AMEN.

Being one with the Lord, you will enjoy all things. Amen.

Prosperity is greatness. Amen.

"Prosper in all things, and you will see that I am with you. Amen."

A lot of what we see is an illusion of what is really there. Amen.

Be wise, and SEE what it is that you need to be seeing. Amen.

"Even when things appear wrong at first, know that I speak that way for a reason."

Much of what is spoken is not just for our growth but for the growth of others as well.

Amen.

The enemy will always attack you with lies, doubts, and illusions. Amen.

This is how the enemy stops you from growing into the Lord. Amen.

Jesus prays for all believers.

In John 17:20–23,

> I do not pray for these alone, but also for those who [a]will believe in Me through their word; that they all may be one, as You, Father, *are* in Me, and I in You; that they also may be one in Us, that the world may believe that You sent Me. And the glory which You gave Me I have given them, that they may be one just as We are one: I in them, and You in Me; that they may be made perfect in one, and that the world may know that You have sent Me, and have loved them as You have loved Me.

About the Author

Greatness Quiroz was born on December 4, 1988, and grew up in a small town by the name of Kermit, Texas. In HIS life, he got married and had five children: three boys and two little girls. Later IN LIFE, Greatness became KNOWN as a prophet by MANY, GOING from place to place and teaching and discovering in Christ Who He really was and for you. He became who he is today by following the Lord Jesus in his life, in his ministry, and just in his forward.